THE
FINEST
ROOMS
in America

THE FINEST ROOMS

in America

Fifty Influential Interiors from the Eighteenth Century to the Present

Thomas Jayne
with Anne Walker

THE MONACELLI PRESS

CONTENTS

9   Introduction

15 TEA ROOM, MONTICELLO
    Charlottesville, Virginia

19 DRAWING ROOM, MILES BREWTON HOUSE
    Charleston, South Carolina

22 LARGE DINING ROOM, MOUNT VERNON
    Mount Vernon, Virginia

27 DINING ROOM, MAGNOLIA MOUND
    Baton Rouge, Louisiana

30 RECEPTION ROOM, VICTORIA MANSION
    Portland, Maine

33 LIBRARY, MARK TWAIN HOUSE
    Hartford, Connecticut

37 DINING ROOM, KINGSCOTE
    Newport, Rhode Island

40 CHINESE BREAKFAST ROOM, THE ELMS
    Newport, Rhode Island

43 COURTYARD, FENWAY COURT
    Boston, Massachusetts

47 GOLDEN STEP DINING ROOM, BEAUPORT
    Gloucester, Massachusetts

51 DRESSING ROOM, VIZCAYA
    Miami, Florida

53 LIVING ROOM, HOLLYHOCK HOUSE
    Los Angeles, California

57 PARLOR CHAMBER, HAMILTON HOUSE
    South Berwick, Maine

59 DINING ROOM, ELIEL SAARINEN HOUSE
    Bloomfield Hills, Michigan

63 CHINESE PARLOR, WINTERTHUR MUSEUM
    Winterthur, Delaware

67   MORNING ROOM, BASSETT HALL
      Williamsburg, Virginia

71   SALA, CASA AMESTI
      Monterey, California

75   LIVING ROOM, MENIL HOUSE
      Houston, Texas

81   LIVING ROOM, CHARLES AND RAY EAMES HOUSE
      Pacific Palisades, California

84   OUTDOOR ROOM, FRANCES BRODY HOUSE
      Los Angeles, California

87   DINING ROOM, THE BIG BEND
      Chadds Ford, Pennsylvania

91   LIBRARY, EDGEWATER
      Barrytown, New York

95   LIVING ROOM, RANDOLPH MARTZ AND GENE WADDELL HOUSE
      Charleston, South Carolina

99   GRAND SALON, THOMAS BRITT APARTMENT
      New York City

100   LIBRARY, STUART AND SUE FELD APARTMENT
      New York City

105   BEDROOM, MARK AND DUANE HAMPTON APARTMENT
      New York City

109   DRAWING ROOM, KENNETH JAY LANE APARTMENT
      New York City

112   WINTER GARDEN, SUSAN AND JOHN GUTFREUND APARTMENT
      New York City

117   LIVING ROOM, CAROLYNE ROEHM APARTMENT
      New York City

121   LIVING ROOM, CANDACE AND FREDERICK BEINECKE APARTMENT
      New York City

126   LIVING ROOM, ROSE TARLOW HOUSE
      Los Angeles, California

131   LIVING ROOM, SUZANNE RHEINSTEIN HOUSE
Los Angeles, California

133   STUDIO, BENTLEY LAROSA HOUSE
Bucks County, Pennsylvania

137   SALON, BETTY BLAKE APARTMENT
Dallas, Texas

140   SALON, FRANCES AND RODNEY SMITH HOUSE
New Orleans, Louisiana

145   BEDROOM/SITTING ROOM, ANNETTE AND OSCAR DE LA RENTA HOUSE
Kent, Connecticut

149   DINING ROOM, OCEANFRONT HOUSE
Palm Beach, Florida

153   LIVING ROOM, VILLA DI LEMMA
Montecito, California

159   LIVING ROOM, KITTY HAWKS HOUSE
Westchester County, New York

164   LIBRARY, FARMHOUSE
Wilmington, Delaware

169   GREAT ROOM, BUNNY WILLIAMS AND JOHN ROSSELLI BARN
Falls Village, Connecticut

173   PARLOR, OAKLEY FARM
Upperville, Virginia

176   LIVING ROOM, ANDREW FISHER AND JEFFRY WEISMAN APARTMENT
San Francisco, California

181   BEDROOM, ALEXA HAMPTON APARTMENT
New York City

185   DINING ROOM, MARY COOPER HOUSE
New Orleans, Louisiana

189   TRIBECA STUDIO
New York City

192   DINING ROOM, ENCINAL BLUFF
Malibu, California

195   DINING ROOM, ROBERT COUTURIER HOUSE
South Kent, Connecticut

199   LIVING ROOM, TRIBECA LOFT
New York City

203   SITTING ROOM, ALBERT HADLEY APARTMENT
New York City

206   Places to Visit

207   Acknowledgments

208   Credits

INTRODUCTION

My earliest consideration of the elements of a refined interior took place in the living room of my parents' house in Pacific Palisades, California, a small postwar filled mostly with family furniture from the nineteenth century. The year I was born, my mother had the room redecorated; the walls were painted in dusty rose to offset plain and patterned teal blue fabrics, and comfortable seating arrangements lay beneath an atmospheric watercolor of Metro Goldwyn Mayer's grand Beaux-Arts studio. Later, her decorator admitted she had used the same scheme in Marilyn Monroe's dressing room, which both horrified and amused my mother. She never used a decorator again, but regardless of how our living room came to be, its comfort, handsome coloration, personal associations, and even its modest size make it one of the finest I have known. Today it is gone, but it was the genesis of a lifetime analyzing what makes a fine room and an appreciation of the value in recording them.

When I left home for the University of Oregon to study architecture and art history, I already had a small collection of books on design, including a first edition of *The Finest Rooms, by America's Great Decorators*, published in 1964. The book's prominent designers included Billy Baldwin, Rose Cumming, Eleanor Brown of McMillen, Michael Taylor, and Sister Parish. Every room was traditional—the style we now call "mid-century" or "modern" was not shown, nor were historic rooms. "This book presents a fabulous cross section of America's most beautiful houses and apartments," the jacket flap reads. "Characteristic of all the interiors is the lived-in, nondecorated look which is the hallmark of the decorators represented here." The book epitomized the taste of the well-to-do in mid-twentieth-century America. Yet by the late 1970s I wanted it for historical, not current, reference, for in the decade following its publication the world of decoration, even traditional decoration, had changed markedly.

My professors fostered my interest in the history of interiors, encouraging me to attend the Attingham Summer School, an intensive, three-week program of private visits to English country houses. Attingham was designed for museum curators and other professionals so the telephone call offering me a place that summer as an undergraduate was distinctly thrilling. Just a few months later I had left my spartan college room behind and was meeting the Duchess of Devonshire in her private

Outdoor room in the Frances Brody House, Los Angeles. Decorated by Billy Haines.

rooms at Chatsworth. That summer I visited more than forty country houses and was steeped in the British design tradition, and subsequently I found myself regularly pondering what constituted the American design tradition.

Later, in graduate school at the Henry Francis du Pont Winterthur Museum and during a fellowship in the American Wing of the Metropolitan Museum of Art, I continued distilling what "American" means, especially in terms of decoration. Winterthur, founded in 1951, is the premier museum dedicated to American decorative arts, and the question "What is American?" is at the heart of the academic effort there.

The lack of a definitive answer, though, is telling. Wendell Garrett, a great expert on American material culture, believes the problem is rooted in the intersection of a variety of cultures here, the stream of immigration, and the amount of change this country has seen in its history. As a result, there is no singular decorative tradition in America. Still, it may be said that some particularly American aspects of design are invention, personal expression, and an unabashed mixture of foreign decorative influences.

At the core of Winterthur's training—and of the consideration of what is American— is connoisseurship of objects and rooms, the result of a process where every object or place is studied and compared to related examples. We learned to ask, "What does this object say about the people who made and used it?" Most of what is preserved at Winterthur contrasts with today's informal lifestyles. Until the mid-twentieth century, Americans employed fashion, houses, and manners to present a formal ideal of refinement, but today comfort reigns. Often the great room—with kitchen, television, and feet-up seating—supplants the parlor, drawing room, and living room of the past. And even when contemporary rooms are elaborate, they are relaxed and flexible, rarely approaching the upright formality of the eighteenth and nineteenth centuries.

Du Pont saw this change, and he wanted to preserve the history of early American life and decorative arts, arranging his vast collection in Winterthur's ninety rooms with painstaking attention to making the decoration of the rooms beautiful. Today, du Pont is recognized as one of America's great influences on interior design and its history. In 1962, First Lady Jacqueline Kennedy asked him to advise on the redecoration of the White House, and he assured the Francophile who favored European decoration that "an American house could be swell."

Albert Hadley's apartment in New York.

Once I had completed my academic training, I decided to become a practitioner rather than a design historian and joined Parish-Hadley, the firm founded by Sister Parish and Albert Hadley, where I apprenticed as David Kleinberg's assistant. Parish-Hadley codified American taste into a sophisticated amalgamation of traditional Anglo-American style, tempered with the influence of twentieth-century Paris. Their rooms were original, inventive, beautifully crafted, and comfortable, and my education in the many refinements of American decoration continued.

At Parish-Hadley, the value of good architecture and architectural detail, as well as the suitability of a room's location and its use, received particular stress. Furniture was selected both for decorative appeal and for the beauty of its construction; while it need not be expensive, it had to be well made. Fabrics were similarly considered, in that they had to represent the best of their type. Color was thoughtfully used, and though both principals liked fresh, bright colors, they were always modulated, never loud. Of primary importance were works of art, whether historically important or simply a reflection of their owner's taste. In fact, I cannot remember a significant room by Parish-Hadley that didn't have at least one meaningful work of art.

Another legacy of my time there is a preference for using the title "decorator," a term reaching back to ancient times, in lieu of "interior designer." Some say interior designers not only decorate but also are responsible for interior architecture. But I suggest that a decorator, in alliance with architects, is also responsible for the architecture of rooms.

The principles instilled through academic training and practical apprenticeship continue to manifest themselves as my own design practice develops. The consideration of quality and authenticity is particularly meaningful to me each time I approach the decoration of a room (as illustrated in the examples above). For me, this formal living room for a collector of American paintings is a tribute to those rooms I first

From the left:
Formal living room
in Dutchess County;
Modern living room
in Southampton;
Territorial-style
sitting room in New
Mexico.

studied in college, for even though it is, as I like to say, archaeologically correct, I have presented a fresh take on a historic style. There is a more modernist approach to the Southampton living room, consonant with the collection of sheets from Matisse's *Jazz* and the Asian ceramics. Similarly, a sitting room at the center of a large ranch in New Mexico is executed in the Territorial style of the American West, with adobe walls and neoclassical details.

This book presents fifty rooms that I know personally, all domestic, representing the best American decoration from the eighteenth century to the present. I hope this volume will serve as a reference work for rooms that exist today. All the rooms are decorated in the classic sense. Some are formal, such as the tea room at Monticello and Frank Lloyd Wright's living room at Hollyhock House, and reflect courtly manners. Others are informal and reflect more the lifestyle of today, such as the living room of the Eames House or Bunny Williams's great room in her Connecticut barn. Some reflect changing tastes in color, with the vivid schemes in the Mount Vernon dining room mellowing into the Colonial Revival decoration at Williamsburg's Bassett Hall and Rose Tarlow's earth-toned living room in Los Angeles.

It is also notable that even within the classic nature of these rooms, the designers could not escape their generation—each room absolutely expresses the decade in which it was created. The dining room at Kingscote could only have been made in the 1880s, and John Saladino's Santa Barbara living room is an archetype of this decade. I have also included among these admittedly grand examples others that are relatively simple because, just as in my parents' house, rooms that are small and not expensive can also be among the finest. I am sure every reader could make worthy additions to this exceptional group, and it is my hope that this book will inspire us all to consider what makes the finest rooms.

TEA ROOM, MONTICELLO

CHARLOTTESVILLE, VIRGINIA

One mantle worn by the multi-talented Thomas Jefferson was that of amateur architect and decorator. At Monticello, his hilltop plantation two miles outside of Charlottesville, he built his dream house, a labor of love that was drawn out over a period of forty years. By 1768, as a young man of twenty-five, Jefferson had begun designing Monticello, and he continued to design, re-design, change, and add to it throughout his life. At a time when the country's architectural identity was just taking shape, Jefferson created a home that was distinctly beautiful, expressive of his intellect and aesthetic, and groundbreaking in terms of American taste. At Monticello, Jefferson drew upon what he admired from architectural books, buildings from antiquity, and particularly European houses and interiors to construct one of America's most iconic buildings.

Thomas Jefferson's tea room at Monticello is a decorative scheme in the true sense of the word. Here in his "most honorable suite," where he displayed on brackets busts of the worthies Benjamin Franklin, John Paul Jones, the Marquis de Lafayette, and George Washington, he achieved a formal and balanced composition of enduring personality through a play of architecture and decoration. Components include an entrance framed by an elliptical arch, two sets of sliding sash doors, a prominent display of a Doric entablature inspired by a building at Albano, Italy, and known to him from Roland Fréart's *Parallèle de l'Architecture Antique avec la Moderne*, and simple but elegant dimity swags and tassels at the windows. Within the classical canon, Jefferson nimbly interpreted the vocabulary to create something inventive and new. His design continues to resonate with modern taste and to delight more than two hundred years later.

Jefferson combined stylish and often imported furniture with simpler pieces made in America and on the plantation. He designed this side table, one of three in the room, after more elaborate French prototypes. The swags and jabots are based on his drawings.

DRAWING ROOM, MILES BREWTON HOUSE

CHARLESTON, SOUTH CAROLINA

With its rich neo-Palladian architecture and opulent decoration, this grand eighteenth-century reception room is undeniably one of the finest rooms in America. Located at the heart of a superb townhouse of the colonial period, it is distinguished by its perfect proportions, carved overdoors, entablature, and a sky blue ceiling, embellished with elegant gilded papier-mâché borders. A portrait by Joshua Reynolds of the original owner and builder Miles Brewton, a successful merchant and one of the largest slave dealers in South Carolina, sits over the beautifully detailed Carrara and Siena marble mantel. Having remained in the same family since it was constructed in the 1760s, the house retains some of its historic furnishings, much of which remains in the original locations. In eighteenth-century fashion, a set of English chairs lines the perimeter of the room—a symmetrical arrangement that reinforces the balance of the architecture. As occasion demanded, the chairs could be moved into convivial groupings. An exquisite English crystal chandelier still holds pride of place. It is a rare example from the eighteenth century, a period when chandeliers were not used in houses because candles were expensive and such an abundant use of them was an extravagance.

New Englander Josiah Quincy Jr. noted in his journal after his visit in 1773:

> The grandest hall I ever beheld, azure blue satin window curtains, rich blue paper with gilt, machee borders, most elegant pictures, excessive grand and costly looking glasses etc . . . At Mr. Brewton's side board was very magnificent plate: a very large exquisitely wrought Goblet, most excellent workmanship and singularly beautiful. A very fine bird kept familiarly playing over the room, under our chairs and the table, picking up the crumbs, etc. and perching on the window, side board and chairs: vastly pretty!

The sky-blue ceiling sets off the lofty proportions of the room and the intricacy of the architectural details, including the pediments, cornices, overmantel, fluted pilasters, delicate Corinthian capitals, and papier-mâché fillets.

LARGE DINING ROOM, MOUNT VERNON

MOUNT VERNON, VIRGINIA

On the shore of the Potomac River sits the majestic Mount Vernon, inarguably one of the most famous houses in America. A soldier, statesman, and gentleman of the eighteenth century, George Washington was keenly aware of the power and meaning of architecture and decoration. He deftly employed a sense of proportion and scale to transform a small ancestral farmhouse into a handsome structure commensurate with his social standing.

The large dining room in the north wing of the house was completed in 1787 after Washington declined the position of king and retired from the presidency to reassume the role of a gentleman farmer. Designed for the level of hospitality Washington's role as a national patriarch and figure of international fame demanded, the room was an unabashed showroom—both richly decorated and grandly scaled. Such a sophisticated display of education and position is rarely made by public figures today, and rooms dedicated not only to making a good impression but also to dining have largely gone out of style. For many, dining rooms are cold, useless, and almost pretentious. However, the Mount Vernon dining room stands timelessly as an example of an impressive room that is both appropriate and engaging through function and spirited decoration. Particularly striking is the vibrant shade of green, a favored and expensive color in the eighteenth century. This bold choice lends contrast to the delicate and stylized plaster ornamentation with agricultural and allegorical motifs including tools, oak leaves, olive branches, and grapevines. While the substantial carved chimney piece, a gift from Samuel Vaughan, a London merchant who immigrated to the United States, was considered by Washington to be almost too elaborate for his republican taste, it anchors the room. The pier glasses were also imported from England, and the furniture was commissioned from the best cabinetmakers in Philadelphia. The large Palladian window, inspired by imported pattern books, amplifies the stately neoclassical nature of the room.

The walls are edged in printed paper and covered in painted green paper, a preferred material and color for dining rooms in eighteenth-century America. The grand mantel features a bas-relief of pastoral scenes and displays a garniture of English vases, also a gift from Samuel Vaughan.

DINING ROOM, MAGNOLIA MOUND

BATON ROUGE, LOUISIANA

This room was built in about 1802 during a vogue for French wallpaper in American rooms. As was typical, relatively restrained neoclassic architectural details frame its elaborate designs. This remarkable paper dynamically unifies the room by connecting the architecture and the other decorative arts. This is a Réveillon design replicated by Brunschwig & Fils and installed in 1995. Also characteristic of American rooms of this period are painted floors and floor cloths—canvases impregnated with painted decorations. The use of paint on floors is both functional and decorative, especially as the color and designs can be discreetly adapted to suit any space. Here, to great effect, a bright red floor cloth serves to highlight the reds and golds in the wallpaper and set off the polished mahogany furniture. Over the table is a punkah, a wooden fan invented in India, which would have been operated by using a rope and pulley.

Magnolia Mound was once the center of a 900-acre plantation on the Mississippi River. It was built as a small settler's house in 1791 and was expanded and aggrandized at the beginning of the nineteenth century in the French Creole taste by Constance Rochon Joyce and Armand Allard Duplantier, a captain of the Continental army under the Marquis de Lafayette, a hero of both the American and French Revolutions.

The restrained architecture—the plain board ceiling and simplified details of the doors and wooden mantelpiece—contrasts with the polished mahogany furniture, the silver, and the giltwood mirror in the room. This is a relationship often seen in early American houses.

RECEPTION ROOM, VICTORIA MANSION

PORTLAND, MAINE

In 1857 hotel entrepreneur Ruggles Sylvester Morse commissioned New Haven–based architect Henry Austin to design an Italianate summer house in Portland and Gustave Herter, later of the fashionable Herter Brothers firm, to carry out the interiors. The rooms of this stately brownstone villa are Herter's earliest known project and, with over ninety percent of the house's original contents still in place, one of his only truly intact commissions. During the thirty-year occupancy of the family of Joseph Libby, founder of the Portland department store, little changed. In the 1940s, William H. Holmes, a retired educator, saved the house, then known as the Morse-Libby House, from demolition and opened it as a museum named in honor of Britain's Queen Victoria.

The lavish and well-preserved reception room is a splendid testimony of America's architectural and decorative aspirations during the pre–Civil War period. Herter conceived of the elaborate space as a whole, decorating it with furnishings of his own design and colorful trompe l'oeil wall paintings executed by leading decorative painter Giuseppe Guidicini. The deft and integrated use of ornament that makes this room a success is the kind that only comes from an artistic eye and the repeated study and use of ornament.

LIBRARY, MARK TWAIN HOUSE

HARTFORD, CONNECTICUT

In 1873 Samuel and Livy Clemens commissioned the well-known architect Edward Tuckerman Potter to design their new home on Farmington Avenue in the Nook Farm area of Hartford, then a center of American culture and home to an influential group of writers and artists. During the 1880s—following the completion of *The Adventures of Tom Sawyer*—the couple secured Louis Comfort Tiffany and his partners in the Associated Artists, Lockwood de Forest, Candace Wheeler, and Samuel Colman, to decorate their public rooms. At that time, the Associated Artists was one of the most important decorating firms in the country, having decorated the Veterans Room at Seventh Regiment Armory in New York. In due time, they would carry out rooms at the White House for President Chester Arthur. Although the family decamped for Europe in 1891, Clemens proclaimed the design integrity of his Connecticut home, writing, "how ugly, tasteless, repulsive are all the domestic interiors I have ever seen in Europe compared with the perfect taste of this ground floor."

The complex shape of the library is centered with the elaborately carved oak mantel, taken specifically for this room from Ayton Castle in Scotland, and the lavish collection of expensive books, unusual objects, and paintings unifies the walls, stenciled with an antique gold-and-blue geometric pattern typical of the Associated Artists. The design of the room is successful in striking the difficult balance between innovation and historicism. Over time, Victorian design has been much maligned and is still generally thought of as unattractive. The library at the Mark Twain House revels in the inventive and enriched beauty of the best of Victorian decoration.

The library served as a backdrop for Twain's recitations of his works in progress for his family and friends. After moving to Europe, he wrote "To us, our house . . . had a heart, and a soul, and eyes to see us with; and approvals and solicitudes and deep sympathies; it was of us, and we were in its confidence and lived in its grace and in the peace of its benediction."

DINING ROOM, KINGSCOTE

NEWPORT, RHODE ISLAND

McKim, Mead & White was responsible for Kingscote's most inspired room—the dining room—which they completed in 1881 for David King Jr. As much a decorator as an architect, Stanford White—to whom the room is attributed—combined a broad spectrum of colors, patterns, textures, and materials to produce an exuberant and whimsical collage in which the line between architecture and decoration is blurred. A master at blending the canonical with the exotic, White ingeniously mixed cork tiles, Siena marble, glazed tiles, carved mahogany, and Tiffany colored glass into a handsomely proportioned composition. The most fantastic aspect of this room, however, is the wall of glass blocks, which allows light to rake inside with ever-changing patterns and colors. White's use of patterned glass in a private house design was entirely innovative. While walls of glass became a common feature of domestic architecture during the next century, the level of artistry and originality exhibited here is unique to this room. The eclectic collection of furnishings, including the oddly proportioned dining chairs, the Italian stands at the fireplace, and the spinning wheel, gives the space an informal air and reinforces its artistic expression.

King was an important trader in Chinese goods, including some of the many ceramics shown on this innovative built-in sideboard. The decoration of this room also relies on Oriental carpets, which were still considered exotic during the latter half of the nineteenth century.

CHINESE BREAKFAST ROOM, THE ELMS

NEWPORT, RHODE ISLAND

In 1901 Horace Trumbauer designed The Elms for Edward J. Berwind, a coal magnate from Philadelphia, and his wife as the couple's seasonal cottage on Bellevue Avenue. Inspired by the Château d'Asnières in Asnières-sur-Seine, the grand Beaux-Arts mansion epitomizes the French taste that thrived in the Gilded Age. At that time, the house was sumptuously decorated by the Parisian firm Allard et Fils and filled with pieces from the Berwinds' collections of Renaissance ceramics, paintings, and jades. With its gilded oak Louis XV–style boiserie framing Chinese lacquered panels from the Kang Hsi period, the breakfast room is a magnificent yet accessibly scaled example of the Beaux-Arts taste. The decoration of this room is a rare survival. Most Beaux-Arts rooms were originally painted and had fabric-covered walls, but due to the fugitive nature of these finishes, they have been repainted or replaced.

COURTYARD, FENWAY COURT

BOSTON, MASSACHUSETTS

Isabella Stewart Gardner, one of the early twentieth century's foremost patrons of the arts, modeled Fenway Court after the Palazzo Barbaro in Venice to embrace her extensive collections of paintings and artifacts—the reflection of her world travels. She disliked the cold, mausoleum-like spaces that defined most American museums and galleries of the period and designed Fenway Court to be a domestic setting to view art. While Gardner lived in an apartment on the fourth floor, she used the rest of the rooms for private events, both artistic and social, and opened her collection to the public for two days a year. Her will created an endowment to make it a public museum.

In 1899, she commissioned Willard T. Sears to design the four-story building on the Fenway centered around this enclosed central court. It has a glazed ceiling supported by steel arches and arcaded masonry composed of architectural fragments, including balconies from the Ca' d'Oro, one of the most beautiful Venetian palazzos on the Grand Canal. The rough walls were sponged with pink and white paint to simulate ancient plaster. Effectively a formal hall without any significant seating or casual elements, the courtyard is an overture to the enriched and formal rooms ahead— a space that was meant to be appreciated as it is passed through. Antique Roman pavement serves as the room's centerpiece. Gardner artfully created a dynamic tension in this space by combining a diverse arrangement of Greek, Gothic, and Asian sculpture with constantly changing horticultural displays. Although there is certainly no other room anywhere like it, this evocative courtyard was greatly influential in shaping American taste and residential design in the years that followed.

The courtyard is centered with a carpet-like combination of Roman mosaic and grass. The shape of the tree ferns echoes the collection of antique columns.

GOLDEN STEP DINING ROOM, BEAUPORT

GLOUCESTER, MASSACHUSETTS

Over a period of twenty-seven years, Henry Davis Sleeper worked with architect Halfdan Hanson to create a diverse and artful assemblage of colonial, French, English, and exotic styles at Beauport, his summer house on the Atlantic Coast north of Boston. Perched on a rocky ledge overlooking Gloucester Harbor, the house was transformed from a cottage into a labyrinthine show house artistically decorated with artifacts, antiques, ceramics, and folk art. A decorator, salvager, and antiquarian, Sleeper was gifted with an eye for arrangement and composition and especially with the ability to find beauty in the patina of age. He has influenced a century of decorators.

The Golden Step dining room, named after an eight-foot China Trade ship model displayed on a wall over a Chinese funerary table, displays Sleeper's brilliant ability to create an enveloping and atmospheric space with assembled and outwardly unrelated furnishings. He often emphasized a specific color as an organizational and decorative device. Here he uses greens and whites to define what he chose to include in the room—for example, English pottery, crystal compotes, Windsor furniture, and glass fisherman's floats. These colors are amplified by the play of light off the harbor, which falls into the room through an expansive window with diamond-shaped panes. Rather than seeming contrived or static, the space is imbued with an impromptu quality as if the party is about to begin.

White walls with green-painted trim bounce the light reflected from the harbor into the room and serve as a foil for the play of various objects and furniture in shades of green.

48

DRESSING ROOM, VIZCAYA

MIAMI, FLORIDA

James Deering, an industrialist who made his fortune manufacturing agricultural equipment, began work on his winter home in Coconut Grove in 1910. To carry out his vision, he worked with Paul Chalfin, the talented New York artist who learned his trade from Elsie de Wolfe and acquired his impeccable taste from Isabella Stewart Gardner. With Chalfin, Deering traveled through Europe searching for inspiration and acquiring architectural fragments, which would eventually find their way into the design of Vizcaya. The Renaissance-inspired mansion overlooking Biscayne Bay was completed in conjunction with F. Burrall Hoffman. Amusingly, the house is centered on a stone breakwater, sculpted to resemble a Baroque barge, that also serves as a terrace.

Deering's bath, brilliantly executed with materials of the best quality, is located on the second floor at the front of the house. The walls of the room are articulated in marble panels of three colors and highlighted by sculpted silver ornaments while a tented ceiling drapes overhead, fashioned from linen with embroidered Pompeian designs. A noteworthy piece of decoration itself, the glamorous shaving stand, shaped like an ancient brazier, serves as a focal point, highlighting the romantic view of the shipwreck and bay beyond. This room is a rare example of high-quality decoration that veers toward extravagance, but its inventive and well-humored spirit lands it squarely in the realm of good taste, making it a particular favorite among designers and decorators.

LIVING ROOM, HOLLYHOCK HOUSE

LOS ANGELES, CALIFORNIA

Built between 1919 and 1921 for oil heiress Aline Barnsdall, Hollyhock House was Frank Lloyd Wright's first project in California. Had the full scheme been realized, the house would have stood as the centerpiece of a theater community with several other buildings on a 36-acre site known as Olive Hill. The fortress-like concrete exterior embellished with abstracted hollyhocks, Barnsdall's favorite flower, belies the open and unexpected living room—the heart of the house. Its monumental nature and formal arrangement of furniture is perhaps due in part to its location in the center of this grand and unexecuted master plan.

With its extreme shapes and novel details, Wright's room showcases the successful dialogue between architecture and decoration. Usually the line between the two is never clear unless a space is completely void of architectural detail and, in that case, it becomes exclusively about decoration. However, the finest interiors always have an architectural personality and, at minimum, fluid proportions. In Hollyhock House's geometrically charged living room, where the interior architecture is extended with furniture designed en suite, it becomes almost impossible to distinguish between the two disciplines. The contours and lines of the pitched vault ceiling, skylights, and built-in benches become decorative elements. Similarly, the enrichment of the fireplace, including an abstract relief of Barnsdall as an Indian princess presiding over her domain and a pool inserted into the heavy stone hearth to reflect the flames, can easily be seen as both architectural and decorative. Conversely, the furniture—especially the sofas, with their architectonic quality—becomes architecture. The gilt screen, built into the wall, becomes part of the volume of the room. It is interesting to consider Wright's great admiration for the compressed qualities of Japanese art in relation to the sculptural depth of his own work. This room is a triumph of Wright's ability to synthesize architecture and interior design.

While Wright was exacting about the arrangement of furniture in his designs, his clients were known for moving it into more practical configurations after he left their houses. One wonders how he imagined the pair of desks, in an almost schoolhouse-like arrangement, would be used.

PARLOR CHAMBER, HAMILTON HOUSE

SOUTH BERWICK, MAINE

At the turn of the twentieth century, Emily Tyson, widow of the president of the
Baltimore and Ohio Railroad, and her step-daughter purchased Hamilton House,
a late-eighteenth-century Georgian building overlooking the Salmon River, as a
summer retreat. Working very much in the Colonial Revival taste, which influenced
so many American rooms at that time, the Tysons renewed the original architecture
and redecorated the rooms in a contemporary style suitable to the space.

In the upstairs parlor chamber—a nod to the old-fashioned term for the best bedroom—the Tysons re-created the wallpaper from original fragments found in the
space. The Chinese matting, which was popular from the early nineteenth century
into the early twentieth century, the bed's white crocheted canopy, and Currier and
Ives prints give the room a sense of comfort and informality. The decorative contrast
of the green opaline glass represents a twentieth-century aesthetic pioneered by
tastemakers such as Henry Davis Sleeper at Beauport. The combination of texture
and scale give the room a particularly American quality. Most certainly, it was
a handsome room when it was built in the nineteenth century and redecorated in
the 1920s but today the historic woodwork and the oxidized papered walls meld
together to give it a level of quality that only the patina of age can create.

DINING ROOM, ELIEL SAARINEN HOUSE

BLOOMFIELD HILLS, MICHIGAN

In 1928, Saarinen began designing his house at Cranbrook Academy, the educational and cultural institution founded by George and Ellen Scripps Booth on their Bloomfield Hills estate as the American equivalent to the Bauhaus. A well-respected architect in Finland, Saarinen immigrated to the United States after winning second place in the Chicago Tribune Building Competition and later took up teaching at the University of Michigan. After the talented professor caught the attention of the Booths, they commissioned Saarinen to design multiple buildings and to oversee the development of the Cranbrook campus. Well-recognized for his romanticism of nineteenth-century Arts and Crafts ideas, Saarinen was also engaged by the Booths as the institution's president and as head of the Department of Architecture and Urban Design. Eliel and his wife, Loja, a successful textile designer, lived in the house until 1950; a full restoration was completed in 1994.

The dining room represents the Saarinens' overarching design ethic: that every aspect of a room should be designed down to the smallest detail to create a unified and coherent picture with a clear connection to the classical past. The shape of the octagonal dining room—embellished with four red corner niches—informs the design of the square rug patterned with concentric octagons and the octagonal base of the table. In turn, the circular tabletop reflects the shape of the lamp and gold-leaf dome. A tapestry by Greta Skogster of birds and trees hangs opposite the French doors leading out to the courtyard. Rendered in elegant and expensive materials, this space reveals what harmonious heights can be reached through inventiveness, creativity, and complication. Here, the Saarinens created a total environment, much as Gustave Herter did at the Victoria Mansion almost seventy years earlier, where the brilliant use of shapes and color result in a balanced design. When both rooms were completed, they epitomized the most tasteful and successful interiors of their generation.

The room is designed down to the smallest detail. In the corner niche is an Eliel Saarinen vase; the curtains are reproduced from fabric designed by his wife, Loja; their son Eero designed the linen placemats; and the table is embellished with a silver-plated sculptural bird attributed to Franz Hagenauer.

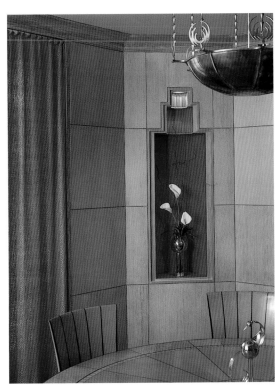

CHINESE PARLOR, WINTERTHUR

WINTERTHUR, DELAWARE

This room stands as the centerpiece of Henry Francis du Pont's house, now the Winterthur Museum, an institution he created "for the education and enjoyment of the public." The intellectually stimulating and visually handsome displays of historic American architecture and decorative arts have been long revered by American scholars. But with his deep interest in interior design, du Pont can easily be considered one of America's great decorators.

The decoration of this room—which du Pont intended for comfort and use—was conceived around a large set of eighteenth-century Chinese wallpaper panels. Hand-painted with a continuous scene of Chinese villagers, this rarity was acquired by du Pont in the 1920s from decorator and historian Nancy McClelland. Chinese wallpaper, fashionable among the American elite in the late eighteenth and early nineteenth centuries, experienced a revival in the early twentieth century. Period rooms at the American Wing of the Metropolitan Museum of Art, opened in 1923, were an important stimulus to this renewed interest. Because the paper at Winterthur was slightly too tall for the space, du Pont specified that the walls be coved in the traditional Regency manner. The scale of the gesture gives the space a twentieth-century, almost Art Deco, feeling. Here, a constraint was transformed into a brilliant solution. Furthering the room's success is the comfortable arrangement of furniture, arrayed for family and friends to gather before dinner. The sofas at the fireplace and the open games table convey a welcoming immediacy. While furnished with the best of Asian-influenced antiques, Chinese porcelains, and lacquered screens, the parlor was designed to be lived in—a modern concept. Du Pont, a disciple of Henry Davis Sleeper, shared Sleeper's strong interest in color as an organizational device. Here, du Pont relies on green, the main shade of the paper, to guide the room's color scheme, glazing the woodwork and selecting damask for the upholstery to match. He placed objects from his collection for decorative contrast. The play of the Derbyshire vases with their purple and brown veining on the mantel against the Chinese papered walls is particularly brilliant. For variety, he maintained several sets of curtains which he changed seasonally; the green and yellow silk sets are still used.

Because Chinese wall-
papers were extremely
expensive in the eigh-
teenth and nineteenth
centuries, they were
used only sparingly
in the smallest rooms.
The use of this paper
on such a grand scale
enforces the twentieth-
century nature of this
room. Du Pont lit the
space with artificial
candles electrified
to simulate the light
levels in which the
furniture was origi-
nally seen.

MORNING ROOM, BASSETT HALL

WILLIAMSBURG, VIRGINIA

Bassett Hall, a two-story eighteenth-century house on 585 acres of gardens and rolling woodlands, represents part of the story of Colonial Williamsburg, a vision financed by John D. Rockefeller Jr. and his wife, Abby Aldrich Rockefeller. In the 1920s the Rockefellers initiated their grand educational plan to preserve and restore an American city to its early appearance. They considered several other cities including New Orleans, but they ultimately chose Williamsburg because of its important historic buildings and its pivotal role in the founding of the United States.

Bassett Hall served as the couple's home during the historic area's early restoration. With an eye for design and unpretentious taste, Abby Rockefeller decorated the interiors to be a home, not a museum, and insisted that the furniture be comfortable by twentieth-century standards and attractive. In their morning room she relied on faded paint colors associated with old finishes, as opposed to the bright colors that later research found to be historically correct. The furniture is all a mellow medium brown and defined, no matter what the specie, as maple. Against the historic architecture, cupboards for china, hooked rugs, some of which she made herself, and, most important, folk art enliven the space. The relative simplicity of this room is even more remarkable given Rockefeller's wealth and his wife's role in the creation of the Museum of Modern Art. And, at the same time, Abby Rockefeller was also one of the pioneers in collecting folk art or the "art of the common man," as she described it.

Inspired by early America, but unhampered by the absolute demands of period authenticity, the Rockefellers created a comfortable, memorable, and, today, art historically important room. Along with many other aspects of Colonial Williamsburg, it is a premier example of the Colonial Revival—or as some have labeled it, the "Williamsburg style"—which greatly impacted the direction of American interior design throughout the twentieth century.

Elements that have decorative value but little to do with early America were regularly found in these so-called Revival interiors, such as the Chinese "jade" tree on the low chest and the nineteenth-century French oil lamps, both of which probably came to America in the twentieth century.

Corner cupboards were pivotal elements in Colonial Revival interiors. In the eighteenth century, they were used to display luxury goods such as ceramics and silver. Later rooms often had multiple examples for expanded collections of these prized objects.

SALA, CASA AMESTI

MONTEREY, CALIFORNIA

At Casa Amesti, the talent of Frances Elkins, one of the early twentieth century's veritable arbiters of taste, is vividly displayed. Elkins purchased the historic but dilapidated 1830s adobe house in coastal Monterey in 1918 and set out to improve it. With her brother, Chicago architect David Adler, she restored the building and brought to the new interiors a sure sense of color, originality, and chic. Fortuitously completed at just the moment when Elkins was considering taking up decorating as her calling, Casa Amesti became a showplace for her burgeoning career, attracting many of her future clients.

In the *sala* (Spanish for living room), Elkins's ability to mix furniture styles and colors into a balanced composition is revealed. The classical details—the dentilated cornice, door casings, and pedimented overmantel—that Adler applied to the space act as a refined and subtle counterpoint to the charming and rustic naiveté of the rough plastered walls and informal planked ceiling. In the Edwardian spirit, Elkins created multiple sitting areas and furniture groupings around a rectangular desk that anchors the geometry of the room. She also deftly used color as an organizing device, relying on a palette of primarily blue and ivory and adding highlights—particularly blue-and-white ceramics and turquoise faience figures—throughout to establish a balance that brings order and confidence to the room.

The combination of objects from many cultures into an artistic whole, pioneered by the Aesthetic Movement, is furthered by Elkins's considered and symmetrical arrangements. This room, decidedly not a Victorian concoction, includes objects from the United States, Britain, France, Italy, Persia, and China.

LIVING ROOM, MENIL HOUSE

HOUSTON, TEXAS

Important cultural figures, collectors, and philanthropists, John and Dominique de Menil asserted their iconoclastic taste with their atmospheric and avant garde home in Houston. In the 1940s, the de Menils relocated from France to Texas; John took on the worldwide operations of the oil services company Schlumberger Ltd., which was founded by his wife's father and uncle. Enthusiasts of modern architecture, the couple commissioned a young Philip Johnson to design a low-slung minimalist brick house with stylish, intellectually charged interiors decorated by fashion designer Charles James that they, in turn, filled with modern works of art.

The living room is a chic open space with polished black tile floors and one jewel-tone wall. While an unlikely choice as decorator, James—who had also designed clothes for Dominique—imbued the sleek Miesian space with a sensuality and texture. The room is a skillful and eclectic mix of various styles of art and furniture, including a curvaceous chaise longue, sculptural chairs, and a seven-sided ottoman, all designed by James. The paintings are the core of the interior, anchoring the antiques and upholstery and balancing the surprising choice of Victorian furniture. Here the sum of the parts creates a decorative whole. Gestures, such as the blue wall, enhance the architectural setting while additions like James's pouf pull the space together. Interestingly, this is an early example of a successful modern interior that relies on eighteenth- and nineteenth-century decorative arts for contrast instead of only using furnishings of the period.

The Victorian Rococo Revival chairs, possibly French, were selected for their sculptural appeal. They may not have seemed unlikely because American Victorian furniture, which was very similar, was especially valued in Texas and other parts of the Southwest because of its association with the region's early settlement.

Dominique de Menil rotated her art collection between her house and the Menil Collection, the museum she built in 1987. This room was particularly well adapted to display different kinds of painting and sculpture without seeming like a gallery. A corner of Mark Rothko's painting The Green Stripe is shown here.

LIVING ROOM, CHARLES AND RAY EAMES HOUSE

PACIFIC PALISADES, CALIFORNIA

Midcentury rooms are often presented as academic set-pieces where all the elements fall into a single time frame—say between 1935 and 1960—and proscribe the tone of the architecture and decoration. In large part due to the way they were first styled for photography, these modern rooms were furnished only with items of recent manufacture to showcase new design. While these images have served as iconic models, they hardly represent the way people usually furnished and lived in these rooms.

In reality, most modern rooms contain a decorative mix of old and new. The Eames house—known as Case Study House #8—was built as one of twenty-five houses as part of *Arts & Architecture's* Case Study program during the mid-1940s and incorporated industrial materials, pre-fabricated members, and off-the-shelf parts derived from wartime America. Charles Eames, a disciple of Eliel Saarinen, and Ray, his second wife, met in 1940 at the Cranbrook Academy of Art where they were both involved in architecture and furniture design. Charles and his design partner Eero Saarinen designed the initial scheme for this house, originally planning to build at the center of the designated site, but that plan was never carried out. Instead, the Eameses, who fell in love with the cliffside meadow overlooking the Pacific, reconfigured the house and placed it on the edge of the property taking advantage of the beautiful views.

The Eameses' double-height living room and studio brings together modern—if not unconventional—architecture with a warm color scheme and the couple's new and antique furniture, candlesticks and ethnic objects, such as textiles and baskets. In contrast to the starkness of so many International Style interiors, this room is packed with personality and texture, obtaining something of the clutter of a Victorian parlor. Tropical house plants enhance the room and fuse the interior of the house with the long vistas of the meadow framed by the glass panels of windows and doors.

Eames designs for
storage furniture are
now highly prized by
decorative arts collec-
tors. The shelving unit
here has an obvious
relationship to the
screen of windows on
the opposite wall.

OUTDOOR ROOM, FRANCES BRODY HOUSE

LOS ANGELES, CALIFORNIA

In the 1950s the great philanthropist and tastemaker Frances Lasker Brody and her husband commissioned Henri Matisse to design a ceramic mural for the interior courtyard of their house, designed by A. Quincy Jones. Brody, known for her discerning eye, did not accept a number of Matisse's first proposals for the space; the artist's initial studies for this commission later came to be some of his greatest cut-out masterpieces. After several renditions, Brody finally approved *La Gerbe*, an organic and free-formed tile mural executed by the ceramic artist Partigas. Paired with the decoration of Billy Haines, this room is both unique and fascinating in terms of its decoration and history. Here, as in Isabella Stewart Gardner's courtyard, art plays a pivotal role in shaping the space and its expression. *La Gerbe* stands as the centerpiece, its bright colors and flowing shapes popping against the solid white brick walls. Comfortable furniture, along with interesting objects such as the ceramic bowl by Picasso, are key to producing the intimate and livable quality of the space. This arrangement contrasts with the formality of the Gardner courtyard, which literally faces the past while the Brodys' looks into the future.

DINING ROOM, THE BIG BEND

CHADDS FORD, PENNSYLVANIA

In the early 1960s, the painter George "Frolic" Weymouth restored an early-eighteenth-century stone Georgian house whose foundations and ground floor were formed out of a seventeenth-century barn. Set within a 180-degree curve of the Brandywine River, this house is known as The Big Bend. Weymouth is an important figure in the artistic community around Chadds Ford, an area made famous by the Wyeths. Related to the great antiquarians Rodney Sharp and Henry Francis du Pont, founder of nearby Winterthur, Weymouth developed his impeccable connoisseurship of American antiques from these cousins. A steward of the area's unblemished landscape and its cultural and natural resources, Weymouth also founded the Brandywine Museum and Conservancy, which now protects 43,000 acres of land.

At The Big Bend, Weymouth turned the house's oldest space—the central room of the barn with thick masonry walls, beamed ceilings, and weathered wood—into a dining room with a seating area and hearth at one end. Effectively, it is one of the earliest rooms in America and perhaps one of the few still in private use. Although the walls and its contents are antique, there are too many furnishings to allow the space to have a period authenticity. Rather, it is a living space very much created by the hand of a collector and arranged for modern entertaining. Here, visual harmony is created by the repetition of forms; the chairs and collections of ceramics are especially pleasing to the eye. In the twentieth century, antiques that were hand-crafted and, as a result, somewhat irregular came to be appreciated for their artistic charm, quirks, and nostalgic associations with the past—perhaps in part a response to industrialization and standardized qualities of mass-produced objects. With its well-worn personality, this room revels in the charm of the antique in an especially sophisticated, artistic, and unique way.

The simplicity of the
furniture forms, the
bare surfaces, and the
minimal upholstery
give this ancient room
a modern quality.

LIBRARY, EDGEWATER

BARRYTOWN, NEW YORK

Built in 1825 by the prominent landowning Livingston family, Edgewater—with its distinctive columned temple front—has been attributed to the talented Charleston architect Robert Mills. The estate's unparalleled location on a small peninsula jutting out into the Hudson River affords quiet seclusion and views of the Catskills. When Robert Donaldson acquired the house in 1852, he commissioned Alexander Jackson Davis to design an octagonal library on the north side of the house. Like Jefferson with his design of Monticello's tea room, Davis and his Victorian contemporaries favored octagonal plans for both their novelty and their economy of construction. During the mid-nineteenth century, this form had an almost cult-like following, a result of a treatise published by the architect and phrenologist Thomas Fowler, but octagonal rooms were never widely embraced because they were difficult to furnish.

However, at Edgewater, this unusual geometry, paired with 26-foot high ceilings and a central octagonal skylight, frames the sophisticated library of Richard H. Jenrette, a steward of old houses. The room was enhanced by the historically informed decoration of Bill Thompson, who used the highest quality American antiques and replicas of nineteenth-century textiles. With the august firm Scalamandré, Thompson created a grandly scaled classical carpet patterned on a ceiling in ancient Pompeii. The genius of the design lies in the juxtaposition of large geometric shapes, repeated by the center table and even the globes, with the polygonal plan of the room. Generally, American libraries became less formal in the later nineteenth and early twentieth centuries, in effect becoming casual sitting rooms. Innovations in printing during the nineteenth century made books more common in houses and hence more difficult to arrange formally. Also, the need for comfortable places to read led to the taste for furnishing these rooms with overstuffed, relaxed pieces deemed unsuitable for formal parlors. This library reminds us of the best qualities of classical rooms dedicated to beauty and books.

The frieze is embellished with a green and gilt border of acanthus leaves, which echoes the colors of the carpet. The white upholstery recedes against the color of the walls, highlighting the furniture, paintings, and architecture.

LIVING ROOM, RANDOLPH MARTZ AND
GENE WADDELL HOUSE

CHARLESTON, SOUTH CAROLINA

In the eighteenth and early nineteenth centuries, Charleston's great wealth provided the means for many fabulous rooms, but after the Civil War and well into the twentieth century, there was much less in the way of formal decorating. During this period, an eclectic range of pieces inherited from various branches of families and mixed with examples of Victorian decoration and European antiques generally defined the furnishings of Charleston rooms. With the city's economic rebirth, decoration is flourishing once again. Ironically, architect Randolph Martz and Gene Waddell, an architectural historian, have responded to this change by evoking the ethos of an old Charleston interior decorated by accretion and association in their living room, which is located in an 1851 house originally designed for two families.

In turning the building into their home, Martz and Waddell removed partitions to create larger spaces. On the second floor, they removed a wall to make one room with regularly spaced nine-over-nine sash windows on three sides—an unusual feature of even the grandest of houses—and retained the side-by-side fireplaces. They made a conscious decision to preserve the old paint for its patina and texture— perhaps in tacit recognition of the famous phase about the origin of Charleston preservation: "Too poor to paint and too proud to white wash." The idea of romance and beauty in decay is an old and sophisticated one. Still, preserving it seems paradoxical with the concept of refinement, unless it is viewed through the artistic eye of an aesthete. Martz and Waddell added a vintage work table, an assortment of nineteenth-century chairs, an unusual Empire-style sofa with a cornucopia and lion's paw feet, and five busts in worn black paint (Augustus Ceasar, Milton, Molière, Cardinal Richelieu, and Voltaire). Coral vines on the outside of the house serve as summer curtains, often balanced by an artful tangle of night-blooming cereus plants—an Amazonian plant once popular in Charleston drawing rooms that blooms only one night a year. Clearly, this room is the remarkable and unique sum of artful subtractions and additions.

By removing a wall
between identical
second-floor front
rooms that were
originally indepen-
dent dwellings, Martz
and Waddell created
a unique version of
the grand second-
floor drawing room
that is ubiquitous in
Charleston. The hole
in the ceiling is a
souvenir of Hurricane
Hugo.

GRAND SALON, THOMAS BRITT APARTMENT

NEW YORK CITY

Brilliantly, this very grand salon in Thomas Britt's Beaux-Arts-style apartment expresses the New York–based designer's willingness to experiment with boldly scaled objects and bright color to create a signature statement. With its luxurious midnight blue satin upholstery, sparking crystal chandeliers, polished black floors, mirrored French doors, and lacquered walls, it is a shimmering and opulent vision rooted in the classical canon.

Falling into the tradition of interiors designed especially for nighttime use, Britt's room is a space whose decoration revolves around the drama of mirrors, candles, and focused artificial light. It conjures the great mirrored galleries of eighteenth-century France and the richly mirrored parlors and drawing rooms in many nineteenth-century houses. But while it epitomizes the glamorous 1970s revival of glittering nighttime rooms fostered by the advent of domestic uplights and so-called can lights for spot and flood lighting, it also luxuriates in the details. The slipper chairs are from Billy Baldwin, the frog-shaped bowls from the estate of Tony Duquette, and the group of bird engravings from Rose Cumming. Exotic objects and artifacts gathered from Britt's travels are interwoven throughout, only adding to the richness and interest of this glamorous space.

LIBRARY, STUART AND SUE FELD APARTMENT

NEW YORK CITY

Stuart and Sue Feld's collection of American paintings is recognized as one of the best in private hands. In their dark green library, they have created what they describe as a "still life of still lifes," artfully arranging works from the third quarter of the nineteenth century within a wall of bookshelves. Basked in the ambient glow of individual picture lights, the room is warm and atmospheric. When the couple acquired Joseph Decker's *Still Life with Apples* eight years ago, they set it on the back of the sofa because the shelves were full. Its informal spot worked so well juxtaposed with the other paintings surrounding it that it has remained there ever since. Magnificent decorative arts are interspersed with the paintings. J. G. Brown's *Picking Apples* is centered above a *secrétaire à abattant* by Duncan Phyfe—there is an identical one in the American Wing at the Metropolitan Museum of Art. William Trost Richards's *Path in the Woods* has pride of place on the wall above the mantel. The Felds have also incorporated one of their other favorite collections into the room—some of the best examples of early lighting, including sinumbra, student, whale oil, and hurricane lamps. Still valued for their sculptural beauty and historic interest, they have been carefully electrified to match the original light levels of burning oil. A rare ingrain carpet with an enriched pattern of reds, browns, and greens supplies the only decorative pattern and visually unites the various and exceptional pieces of the room into an engaging living still life.

Stuart Feld was one
of the first to advocate
using frames related
to the date and style
of a painting, which
is now accepted as the
best way to display
art. This group of both
original and replica
frames works as a
group and harmonizes
with the linear quality
of the bookcases.

BEDROOM, MARK AND DUANE HAMPTON APARTMENT

NEW YORK CITY

The late Mark Hampton, one of the luminaries of the interior design world, began his career as the New York representative of David Hicks, then the most fashionable decorator in England. After working at Parish-Hadley and McMillen, he ventured out on his own in 1976. This bedroom in his family's apartment, still used by his wife, Duane Hampton, encapsulates Hampton's talent for making rooms seem fresh within an established vocabulary and creating innovative spaces anchored in tradition. Here, the decorative scheme is established by the silver-ground Chinese paper painted with branches and birds. Hampton had the vision and courage to literally roll the panels of paper into balls to crease it, a risk that created a semblance of age and irregular surfaces to refract light. This is something that only the most confident of decorators would attempt. Valences interpreted from designs in Regency pattern books reflect Hampton's, as well as his mentor Hicks's, take on period geometries; the bed is draped en suite. The crisp curtain silhouettes and remarkable wallpaper frame this beautiful room, which shows, as Hampton once said, that tradition does not go out of style.

The Hamptons sub-
scribed to the notion
that bedrooms are the
best place for cherished
personal possessions,
as expressed by the
groupings of framed
photographs and the
triangular table, a
memento from their
first apartment, which
they literally found
on the street and
painted white.

DRAWING ROOM, KENNETH JAY LANE APARTMENT

NEW YORK CITY

The drawing room of jewelry designer Kenneth Jay Lane's apartment occupies the piano nobile of a townhouse originally designed by Stanford White in 1898 for banker and state senator J. Hampden Robb and his wife, Cornelia Van Rensselaer Robb. With its fifteen-foot walls and elaborately carved plaster ceiling, it is a soaring and architecturally distinct space that still echoes the influence of the Gilded Age. Here, Lane has created a remarkable and asymmetrical balance of the carefully considered and the seemingly impromptu—a carryover from nineteenth-century decoration. With its collection of paintings, the room calls to mind the jumbled and cluttered nature of artists' studios, such as that of William Merritt Chase. Dark brown walls set off the room's architectural heritage, creating an atmospheric backdrop for Lane's mix of patterns and layers of furniture, including needlework-covered Louis XV chairs, animal-print upholstery and throws, ottomans, Persian carpets, and Regency pieces. Lane's eye for arrangement extends to the jam-packed array of artifacts, ephemera, and books. As this room aptly displays, a fine room does not necessarily have to be perfectly ordered in every detail.

The ornate plaster-
work of the ceiling,
an unornamented
element in most rooms,
forms a perfect archi-
tectural balance with
the imposing mantel.
Busts of Mars and
Athena stare down on
the profusion of works
of art in the space,
which is centered by
a comfortable double-
sided sofa.

WINTER GARDEN, SUSAN AND JOHN GUTFREUND APARTMENT

NEW YORK CITY

Known as the Winter Garden, this room is built around eighteenth-century painted panels from a Belgian chateau and an abundance of potted plants. Not only does it have all of the typical elements of a garden room, it is remarkably well crafted, making it memorable for both its beauty and its quality.

Authored by the great Henri Samuel and Susan Gutfreund, who is a decorator herself, this room contains a combination of upholstered chairs by the august firm Gael de Brousse, antique hand-painted doors (contributed from Samuel's own collection), an English earthenware mantel, and a Russian Bessarabian rug. One of the deans of French design, Samuel is considered a legend. His commissions include rooms for nobility and royalty, Rothschilds, Vanderbilts, and the couturier Valentino. Here, he adroitly combines a collection of historic architectural elements and period furniture to make a truly sumptuous room. It is a combination that could easily overwhelm if it had not been done with the delight of whimsy and a mature sense of what makes a complete and comfortable room. This romantic atmosphere is contained in one of New York's most elegant apartment buildings, a rich neoclassic essay by architect Rosario Candela, with splendid views of Central Park.

Gutfreund and Samuel successfully integrated a range of elements into this bright, sunlit room, including an eighteenth-century clock, a Russian chandelier, and a Diego Giacometti table.

LIVING ROOM, CAROLYNE ROEHM APARTMENT

NEW YORK CITY

The decoration of a double-height room is a classic challenge in interior decoration. By virtue of the golden mean, this type of space often benefits from perfect proportions but for obvious reasons, most of the furniture—and hence decoration—must remain close to the floor. Without the benefit of a great cycle of murals, such as those in Palladian villas, or enriched walls, like those in the double-cube room at Wilton, the decoration is difficult to balance.

In this double-height living room in one of the city's grand studio buildings—designed by Caughey & Evans in 1930—Carolyne Roehm has met the challenge of decorating such a space by keeping the placement of furniture relatively spare, highlighting the woodwork with bright glossy white paint, and choosing a rich brown for the walls. This refined setting is further lightened by the absence of personal items such as groups of family photographs, stacks of books and personal ephemera, which Roehm displays elsewhere in the apartment. The decor follows the traditional styling of formal reception or drawing rooms, established in eighteenth-century Europe, as neutral foils for those occupying the room. Here, the overriding element of good taste and reflected decorum of its creator gives this room personality and elegance.

Slender pilasters with flattened Ionic capitals rise the full height of the room while the wall surface is broken up by double-hung paintings and door openings with abstracted balustrades above.

LIVING ROOM, CANDACE AND
FREDERICK BEINECKE APARTMENT

NEW YORK CITY

This grandly scaled living room, located in a historic McKim, Mead & White building on Fifth Avenue—the first luxury apartment building to rise along the thoroughfare—is home to a couple who collects wonderful objects. Many collectors arrange their treasures in unembellished rooms, working with the preconceived notion that their works of art can stand on their own—that decoration might detract from their force. This interior revels in great collections of fine and decorative arts and well-conceived decor.

A large portrait of the Bourbon del Monte Family by Podesti, painted circa 1829, immediately infuses the room with life while an eighteenth-century Aubusson carpet anchors the space and provides rich color and texture. At center hangs a rare and remarkable Viennese chandelier, circa 1810, and a suite of Louis XVI furniture, attributed to Jacob, one of the greatest of all furniture makers, is arranged around it. These pieces easily impress those who enter the room, but the high quality and subtle coloration of the decoration mellows their effect, making the art seem at home rather than on display. The space unfolds similarly to Isabella Stewart Gardner's Fenway Court, unveiling great art in a sympathetic domestic setting. The painted border on the ceiling echoes and enhances the colors of the carpet, and the beautifully proportioned curtains—one layer of sheer batiste and two layers of unlined silk taffeta—allow for privacy and filtering of light. Notably, the silk velvet upholstery has been covered with slipcovers, not only making the furniture more accessible and comfortable but also abridging their scale to relate to the other works of art.

While the Beineckes have occasionally sought counsel from designers and craftsmen, in the end, this interior was personally composed and realized by them. Clearly, they understand the relationship between beautiful works of art and decoration in creating a memorable and livable room.

When this room was decorated, the mantel appeared, to the contemporary eye, underscaled for the space. Since it is an original feature, the effort was made to keep it. The French mirror, signed Mesnard and dated 10 June 1765, and a remarkable pair of Austrian neoclassical gilt wood sconces beautifully balance it.

While the chandelier has been artfully electrified with very small lights, it also still burns candles. The seventeenth-century French bronze of Apollo and Daphne has been placed in the window to catch the natural light. The border of the carpet is reflected in the design of the painted ceiling.

LIVING ROOM, ROSE TARLOW HOUSE

LOS ANGELES, CALIFORNIA

Some of the best American rooms are analogous to the best of American fashion: tailored, durable, somewhat novel with a hint of glamour. This room from the Bel Air house of Los Angeles–based furniture designer and decorator Rose Tarlow has all of these qualities. While importing antique parts and pieces to compose spaces is not a new concept—Stanford White was a leading proponent, for example— Rose Tarlow forges a new angle on an age-old tradition. She relies on simpler and often rustic architectural elements and objects—old but not ornate. This emphasis gives a timeless and almost abstract quality to the space, created by the juxtaposition of shapes and surfaces. Here, the crossbeams of the ceiling, taken from an eleventh-century church, are combined with examples from the seventeenth century. An antique mantel is flanked by rough-hewn wood-paneled doors. These elements are unified by rough white walls decorated with trailing vines that have seemingly crept in from the outside—a combination of materials that refers, at least obliquely, to California's Spanish Colonial Revival taste. Tarlow also softens the formal balance of the space by casually arranging her personal effects: newspapers hang on ladder rungs and paintings are propped up rather than hung. This is a room with a unique and beguiling sense of place.

The arrangement of the window wall with its deep reveals and recessed bookcases provides both architectural detail and mass for the room. The chairs are representative of the furniture Tarlow designs after eighteenth- and nineteenth-century models.

LIVING ROOM, SUZANNE RHEINSTEIN HOUSE

LOS ANGELES, CALIFORNIA

One of the great themes of decoration today is the reinterpretation of traditional design in renewed or fresh ways. The term transitional—between antique and modern—has been coined to name this trend. Suzanne Rheinstein makes the very best of this type of decoration. Raised in New Orleans and now living in California, she strikes a successful balance using references to the old South to create something contemporary in the front room of her Los Angeles house. Almost everything in the room is old: the architecture, the furniture—mostly Regency and Victorian—and the works of art all date to before 1920. And in Edwardian fashion, the furniture is traditionally arranged into seating groups. Yet, the matched slipcovers in a wide blue-and-ivory stripe, both elegant and practical, unify the space in an up-to-date way, distancing it from the appearance of a historic parlor or living room. What is a completely old-fashioned throwback is that the room is only used for parties. Rheinstein understands the luxury of having a comfortable, welcoming space that is always ready for special occasions—indeed a luxury in this age of the multi-use room.

STUDIO, BENTLEY LAROSA HOUSE

BUCKS COUNTY, PENNSYLVANIA

Many great rooms have been created around a singular object, as is exemplified by this room in a house owned by Ronald Bentley and Salvatore LaRosa, partners at the architecture and design firm B Five Studio in New York.

To showcase this antique Belgian bed, Bentley and LaRosa created a modern room charged with a personal aesthetic that eschews many of the tenets of contemporary design—hard-edged, white, and unornamented. This room has a streamlined quality created by strong horizontal elements and relatively simple details. While these aspects contrast with the upright nature of the bed, they complement its quality and weight. At the same time, the curved desk chair adds to this dynamic play of shapes and dimensions. The walls of green Venetian plaster—which mirror the greenery outside the picture window—and the color of the architectural wood set off the sculptural quality of the bed.

The designers' fasci-
nation with horizontal
lines is reinforced by
the cantilevered bed-
side shelf. The draped
table is an unexpected
element that serves
as something of a full
stop in a composition
based on horizontal
elements.

135

SALON, BETTY BLAKE APARTMENT

DALLAS, TEXAS

A doyenne of Dallas society and an important patron of the arts, the East Coast–descended Betty Blake first came to Texas in the 1940s and made it her home. In 1951 she opened the state's first contemporary art gallery; she is dedicated to emerging artists and has strongly supported museum development, especially the Modern Art Museum of Fort Worth.

Blake's apartment, located in a midcentury building in Turtle Creek, is a vibrant testimony to its creator's style and daring intuition. It is a perfect balance of quality, color, risk, modern, and classic. With the help of Fort Worth–based decorator Joseph Minton, Blake employed white walls and floors to create the ideal backdrop for her personal art collection, including paintings and sculpture by William T. Wiley, Jeff Koons, Mario Shinoda, Jose de Rivera, and Alfred Jensen, and an assemblage of furniture that includes Louis XV chairs, a Saarinen table and, at center, a suite of pieces designed by Syrie Maugham. Famous for designing all white rooms—some say the first—Maugham also enjoyed using color. With an ironic note, Blake has covered her sofas with bright pink upholstery and red and blue decorative bows and placed them in her own white room.

SALON, FRANCES AND RODNEY SMITH HOUSE

NEW ORLEANS, LOUISIANA

At their home, the Smiths, owners of Soniat House—the French Quarter's most celebrated and stylish boutique hotel—created a glamorous and effusive refuge that falls into the rich and worldly tradition of interior decoration in the American South. The townhouse, built in the 1860s, was restored by Frank Masson, the renowned New Orleans restoration architect. The salon, sumptuously decorated by London-based designer Nicholas Haslam, is appointed with a gleaming South American purple-wood floor, gilded chinoiserie wallpaper handpainted by Paul and Janet Czainksy of London, and two *verre églomisé* mirror panels executed by Czech-born artist Nominka d'Albanella. Floor-length ashes-of-roses silk curtains, representing the ongoing tradition of beautiful and elaborate curtains in southern decoration, add drama to the space. A melange of antiques, reflecting many of the cultures that shape New Orleans—an English neoclassical sofa, French bergères, and American side chairs—combined with exotic textiles, all of great quality, form a room with a genius of place and an international point of view.

The handpainted
gilded wallpaper
creates a glowing
backdrop to the eclectic
array of furnishings
and bright color used
in the room while a
large chandelier with
an abundance of
orange candles serves
as a centerpiece for
the space.

BEDROOM/SITTING ROOM, ANNETTE AND OSCAR DE LA RENTA HOUSE

KENT, CONNECTICUT

In private rooms, such as bedrooms and sitting rooms, it is difficult to create a beautiful and inviting space on a large scale. With great style, Annette and Oscar de la Renta achieved this delicate balance at their house in Connecticut with their deluxe multipurpose room that functions as a sitting room, library, and bedroom. Architect Ernesto Buch discreetly organized the space to accommodate its many uses, designing it around a central Palladian window, with views to the de la Rentas' celebrated gardens, twelve-over-twelve windows allowing for ample light, and a wooden mantel patterned after one of Lord Cholmondeley's at Houghton. At once grand and livable, the room also features a fine balance of stately proportions, architectural detail, and comfortable practicality. Corinthian columns, bold cornices, and walls painted shades of white and sienna to resemble stone give rise to its grand, almost aristocratic expression. A selection of well-scaled antiques—including an eighteenth-century table by William Kent, a black-lacquer Chinese export table, and Louis XVI bergère—comingle with piles and shelves of books and soft, inviting sofas. Most impressive is the early-Georgian-style bed with embroidered hangings, set into an alcove created by a pair of bookcases. This remarkable example of the decorative arts encapsulates both the architecture and the decoration of the room.

Stacks of books and the
seemingly impromptu
arrangement of the
Baltic desk are casual
elements that offset the
formality of the archi-
tecture. Louis XVI
chairs and a richly
carved console table
mix with comfortable
armchairs draped
with throws.

DINING ROOM, OCEANFRONT HOUSE

PALM BEACH, FLORIDA

While Palm Beach has some of the most important examples of domestic architecture in the country, it also has a seaside vibe where the best of the houses feature glorious detail combined with the comforts of oceanfront living. In the case of this dining room, located in a historic Marion Sims Wyeth–designed house from 1938, the hostess proudly asserts that you can sit on any chair in a wet bathing suit. When the house, which has been in the family since the 1960s, passed from family matriarch to the next generation, the new owners brought in Thad Hayes to reconceive the interiors for modern family living and to bring it gently into the twenty-first century.

Hayes brought a new sense of life to the dining room and at the same time remained true to its prior expression. Hayes is well known for his calm modern palette, edited reserve, and ability to mix furniture and elements of different periods and styles. This room is no exception. Against the backdrop of Wyeth's Colonial Revival architecture, he continued the narrative of the house by reproducing vintage wallpaper, but he has added Art Deco pieces, including a 1940s French mirror, alongside a pair of inlaid Italian commodes, early American furnishings, and a modern Italian chandelier, for interest and variation. This arrangement is artistically set against the walls. Hayes commissioned Gracie to replicate the original 1930s wallpaper with grisaille floral motifs, a broad stroke that places the room within the continuum of history but also gives it a beautiful and fresh appearance.

LIVING ROOM, VILLA DI LEMMA

MONTECITO, CALIFORNIA

The work of John Saladino best represents the influence of the Mediterranean derived from the classical and Renaissance traditions. Unlike many American decorators who prefer the Anglo-American style and its contrasts of large-patterned printed fabrics, eighteenth-century English furniture, and small-scaled rooms, Saladino, with his artistic vision and scholarly knowledge of Italy and the Iberian Peninsula, has done much to further the so-called Spanish Colonial or Mediterranean Revival. Flourishing in the United States at the beginning of the twentieth century, this style emerged with the development of the Far West and suited its architectural tradition and climate. As the location of one of the most beautiful Spanish missions in the country, Santa Barbara, with its southern exposure toward the Pacific Ocean and subtropical temperature, was an epicenter of its reemergence.

In the Montecito section, Saladino discovered a dilapidated 1920s stone house, which he has lovingly restored. In his living room, he mixes seventeenth- and eighteenth-century Italian, Spanish, and Iberian furniture, pieces he admires for their strong forms and richly textured fabrics—especially velvets and damasks. He only uses textiles with small patterns, which acquire an almost jewel-like quality against the robust texture of the solid masonry walls. In what he describes as a walk-in still life, he demonstrates his genius for theatrical arrangement, his decoration playing against the monumental construction, grandly scaled twelve-foot ceiling, and giant fireplace. His traditional upholstered furniture, slenderized with an eye toward modern Italian design, can be arranged in various configurations depending on the event. Here, he ascribes to the rules of American comfort, deftly combining them with a Mediterranean vernacular to create a beautiful room that is both rustic and refined.

Antique candlesticks
and sconces fitted for
electricity illuminate
this room. In addition
to their sculptural
quality, Saladino
admires the nuanced
lighting they produce
and the fact that the
repetition of their
slender forms does not
overpower the space.

154

Much of Saladino's decoration involves strategically placed artifacts for both intellectual and artistic interest. As one enters the room from the hall, there is a long view to an antique column in the far corner, which metaphorically serves as a pivot for the decoration of the room.

LIVING ROOM, KITTY HAWKS HOUSE

WESTCHESTER COUNTY, NEW YORK

Kitty Hawks feels her work is not premeditated—a quality that gives her decoration an informal and spontaneous character. Nevertheless, her designs also represent a lifetime of seriously considering beauty, comfort, and history. This continued study underpins each of the rooms she decorates.

An important moment in her understanding of interior decoration occurred when she visited Blenheim as a teenager with her mother, Slim Keith. There, amid the eighteenth-century ducal splendor of one of Britain's largest and grandest country houses—in fact a palace—she discovered comfort and thought, "If it was possible to create comfort in that kind of setting, there would be no excuse not to do it everywhere." Many of the inviting qualities Hawks admired at Blenheim reflect the efforts of Consuelo Vanderbilt, the American heiress who was married to the ninth Duke of Marlborough. A woman of great style and personality, she remodeled and redecorated parts of Blenheim after the luxurious and modern comforts of The Breakers, her parents' house in Newport.

Hawks's own living room in Westchester County, New York, is generously scaled and gracefully arranged. It was designed around her mother's framed nineteenth-century wallpaper panels with views of a zoo filled with exotic animals. Her mother had used them in her house in England and later in her Long Island residence. Their history, artistic quality, and informal nature represent for Hawks all the ingredients of a successful room. To complement them, she designed curtains and shades in a chintz in a related color palette. The room is deliberately arranged with comfortable places to sit among a diverse array of treasures both inherited and collected.

The casual arrangement of upholstered furniture, covered in three types of fabric—chintz, Fortuny, and plaid—contrasts with the simpler lines of the room.

The large chaise and lamp with a smaller stool and table illustrates Hawks's ability to arrange furnishings of different scales and styles.

LIBRARY, FARMHOUSE

WILMINGTON, DELAWARE

The venerable Anglo-American tradition in decorating, including the use of printed textiles—especially chintz—and furnishing with antiques and relaxed overstuffed furniture, is represented by this library of an eighteenth-century farmhouse. Decorated by Vivien Greenock, a veteran of the august London firm Colefax and Fowler, the room is centered by beautifully crafted sofas upholstered in linen embellished by a chinosiere pattern. Printed textiles in American interiors began with Asian imports in the early eighteenth century and became universally popular in the early nineteenth century with the perfection of roller printing in England and France. However, chintz, which was especially fashionable in the 1980s, has foundered almost to the point of extinction, and printed linens with similar patterns have taken its place. The texture of the linen mutes and softens the edges of the design, appealing to the current taste for less color and contrast. Here, Greenock has subtly combined linen with other printed and embroidered fabrics throughout the room, including the Turkish Suzani, typical of the Colefax and Fowler style, covering the ottoman.

The antiques, including a handsome needlework-covered wing chair, tables made from drums, English pottery squirrels and Chinese export paintings, only enhance the charm of the architectural surroundings created by the old stucco walls with deep set windows, large fireplace and original fielded paneling. Often relaxed rooms are not considered refined; however, here the subtle combination of printed and embroidered fabrics, needlework, and antiques and the art come together beautifully, demonstrating that a room can be both comfortable and sophisticated.

The English Country House

GREAT ROOM, BUNNY WILLIAMS AND
JOHN ROSSELLI BARN

FALLS VILLAGE, CONNECTICUT

With the vision of a collage artist, Bunny Williams and her husband, John Rosselli, have the ability to combine seemingly unmatched elements of interior decoration into pleasing and comfortable rooms. They see, better than almost all of us, the subtle connections between different objects, both old and new, or grand or simple, and can arrange them beautifully. This talent is revealed in the 1840s hay barn on their property in Connecticut. Designed as a place ideal for entertaining, this memorable 30-by-50-foot room retains its hand-hewn post-and-beam frame and wide floor boards, but as a foil to its rustic construction, Williams and Rosselli added arched windows and an elegant mantel.

To furnish their barn, Williams and Rosselli employed classic decorating devices for making guests feel cosseted. There are comfortable places to sit and to have a conversation. They practice, and probably helped invent, the rule that every guest should have a place to set a drink. Key to the success of the room is its attractive mix of informal Italian, English, and French furniture carefully chosen over time to fit the scale of the space and to have a visual relationship in shape, color, and texture.

All of this creates a unique and special place that is immediately hospitable. Its appearance of all being so effortlessly and organically put together is a testimony to Williams and Rosselli's skill as decorators.

In their barn, Williams and Rosselli created an expansive space that contrasts the small rooms of their nineteenth-century farmhouse. A large marble-topped table, which Rosselli uses as a desk, and over-scaled Italian chair are prime examples of the grand furniture they chose to fit the proportions of the room.

PARLOR, OAKLEY FARM

UPPERVILLE, VIRGINIA

Oakley Farm is centered by an Italianate villa in the heart of Virginia's hunt country. Built in 1857, the house was based on the popular pattern book *The Modern Architect* by the Philadelphia architect Samuel Sloan. Having descended through several generations of the same family, the house and its rooms, last decorated in the 1960s by Sister Parish, needed renewal when the property passed to the present owners. Because the interior architecture had never been fully finished, Peter Pennoyer Architects was brought in to refine the details, adding appropriate moldings, cornices, and decorative ceilings throughout. Katie Ridder decorated the rooms, demonstrating her understanding that mid-nineteenth-century architecture still has much appeal, especially if presented in a contemporary and fresh way. Victorian decoration of that period, with its surfeit of multicolored and patterned walls of fabric, heavily draped windows, and formal furniture—often with prickly horse-hair covers—is for the most part considered undesirable.

In this parlor, Ridder chose to create decoration that obliquely referenced the original period of the house and sat well with the nineteenth-century style of the architecture. More important, she chose to reflect the tastes of the young family who lives in the house, employing a simplified scheme of just two colors and incorporating new upholstered furniture based on nineteenth-century models covered with contemporary fabrics. For the curtains, rather than use the rings and poles standard in most rooms today, she evoked the outline and scale of Victorian curtains with new pelmets embellished with giltwood twigs and embroidered with flowering branches by Penn and Fletcher—a flourish that nods not only to its Victorian predecessors but also to the rural setting of the house. She included antique low tables, also with gilded branches, and lampshades with fanciful leaves to bring the room into the present. Meanwhile, the family's historic portraits—an essential counterpoint to the design—enhance the room's sense of continuity.

The use of an Oushak carpet further updates this room from its Victorian precedents. Oushak carpets first became favored by American decorators in the 1960s and 1970s. Compared to dense and dark Persian carpets that were previously popular in America, they appear more relaxed with looser so-called tribal designs and brighter colors.

LIVING ROOM, ANDREW FISHER AND JEFFRY WEISMAN APARTMENT

SAN FRANCISCO, CALIFORNIA

In California, there is a great and often overlooked tradition of interior design infused with expansive scale and glamour, in part a response to its location in the Far West and in part due to the influence of Hollywood. The tangible history and evidence of this design aesthetic is slight because few of these marvelous rooms, even those from a decade ago, have survived, save in photographs and in motion pictures. This Nob Hill living room with sweeping views of San Francisco owned by decorator Jeffry Weisman and his partner, artist Andrew Fisher, captures the ambience of this tradition with a setting of great mirrored walls—antiques from Germany—combined with objects from great Californian decorators. For example, column capitals from the estate of Michael Taylor serve as cocktail tables and many elements in the space were gifts from Tony Duquette. Adding to this eclectic and comfortable mix are a variety of well-chosen antiques, velvet upholstery, Russian side chairs with fabric woven from peacock feathers, and Fisher's own furniture concoctions, including a walnut and gilded steel side table. All of this is combined into a fantastic and evocative room.

An eighteenth-century Portuguese mirror, a gift from the late Tony Duquette, hangs above the French mantel. The room also includes one of Fisher Weisman's glass lamps and a whimsical shell encrusted chair paired with an eighteenth-century Italian desk.

179

BEDROOM, ALEXA HAMPTON APARTMENT

NEW YORK CITY

Alexa Hampton imparts her deep interest in the history of decoration, an interest shared with her late father, the decorator Mark Hampton, in her New York City bedroom—a prewar space distinguished by an elegant vestibule entrance, short flight of stairs and steel casement windows. Hampton admires the theatricality and comfort of David Hicks's canopy beds and has deftly emulated them here with a suggestion of historic bed hangings. Charles de Beistegui's remarkable manner of displaying of works of art in the Château de Groussay in France has informed her arrangement of drawings by her father with her own. Hampton has successfully translated these influences in a fresh and stylish way, at the same time maintaining the qualities of what a bedroom should be—practical and comfortable. The room has generous bedside tables with shelves for books and a slipper chair in slate-colored upholstery which subtly contrasts the quiet and contemporary color scheme of white and gray. The streamlined bolection-style mantel and artwork above adds to the sleek and crisp atmosphere.

Hampton says that she is less formal than her father and very much of her own generation. Indeed, this room reveals her ability to combine her historic inheritance with a relaxed and modern quality that beautifully resonates with the taste of today.

Hampton adjusted the scale of the bed to make this especially large bedroom seem more intimate. While the books, works of art, and photographs give the room a unique personality, it resonates with a neutral and calm feeling as a refuge from the outside world.

DINING ROOM, MARY COOPER HOUSE

NEW ORLEANS, LOUISIANA

Artistic judgment is perhaps the most important basis of every fine room. Proof of this notion is embodied in the dining room of Mary Cooper, an artist and professional chair-caner, in her early-nineteenth-century Creole house in the Bywater neighborhood of New Orleans. Here, she and her husband purposely live a simpler life reflective of former times, reliant on candlelight and fans. This space, originally added as a utility shed in the late nineteenth century, now acts as a hyphen between the original house and the kitchen, serving both as an entry and a dining room. Furnished with unassuming objects, its refinement is achieved though the play of texture, color, and arrangement. Cooper maintains the distressed and rustic character of the weatherboard walls and board-and-batten shutters, highlighting the fact that the space was once open to the exterior. She uses her gift as a colorist to successfully wash the room in periwinkle and chartreuse, a difficult combination of colors. Notably and coincidentally, the great decorator Elsie de Wolfe did recommend a similar palette to suggest antiquity. Despite the hard-edged quality of the room with its set of upright antique chairs and a long cypress table formed from a single plank, it exudes a distinctive warmth, style, and sense of comfort.

For Mary Cooper,
the selection and
arrangement of every-
day objects is part of
her artistic endeavor.
The table with sat-
sumas and a bottle of
their juice and even
the kitchen beyond,
with highlights of
red enamel, are
carefully considered
compositions.

TRIBECA STUDIO

NEW YORK CITY

Christopher Coleman uses an enriched modernism to fill his rooms with personality. When gray rooms first became popular in the 1970s, they were largely based on matching gray flannel walls and industrial carpeting with white for contrast. At that time, some designers, such as Thomas Britt, experimented with very dark rooms, and a few even with black rooms, notably Albert Hadley's bedroom for Oatsie Charles.

Most designers are too afraid of the sobering effects of black to use much of it in decoration. Coleman is obviously not. In this apartment, he has used it much as gray was used in the 1970s and as a foil for the almost playful spirit of the room. This liveliness is created by a rich combination of geometries juxtaposed with the rounded edges of the furniture, objects, and works of art: the plaid window panels, a freeform wall sculpture, the three types of lighting devices, a tufted day bed, and a shaped lounge chair, for example. Set against black and white, these furnishings literally play off each other and take the room away from the hard-edged feeling typical of modernist interior design.

ALWAYS YIELD TO
TEMPTATION
BECAUSE IT MAY
NOT PASS
YOUR WAY AGAIN

*Coleman sectioned off
the bedroom nook in
the studio with silver
beaded curtains. The
bold graphic nature
of the artwork rein-
forces the graphic
quality of the decora-
tion, from the black-
and-white square
curtain hangings,
low bookshelves, and
pillows.*

DINING ROOM, ENCINAL BLUFF

MALIBU, CALIFORNIA

The dining room at Encinal Bluff, a commodious oceanfront house, embodies
personality on a grand scale. Designed by architects Ferguson & Shamamian and
decorated by Michael S. Smith, the room represents the merging of high-quality
architecture and decoration. With a handsomely coffered ceiling, lofty proportions,
and monumental bronze-sashed doors onto the ocean, the room is well designed
to accommodate the decor, especially the pair of eighteenth-century Flemish
chandeliers and the side cupboard with oyster veneer that was owned by Bill Blass,
a renowned designer of fashion and of great interiors.

The art of the decorator is very much in evidence. Smith commissioned additional
Georgian-style chairs to fill out an incomplete set; these provide a welcome rhythm
of repetition and add to the charm of the antique, a quality that is reinforced by
the large table, crafted from old bogwood, which centers the room. Meanwhile, the
apple-wood matting, suitable to the ocean setting, creates a subtle contrast while
the unexpected placement of the Asian lanterns beneath the console tables adds
a welcome bit of confident good humor.

DINING ROOM, ROBERT COUTURIER HOUSE

SOUTH KENT, CONNECTICUT

Here French-born architect and interior designer Robert Couturier evokes his native taste within the context of an early-eighteenth-century American house with later additions and outbuildings built to his designs, which form his New England country retreat.

The dining room, added in 2009, speaks to these old buildings and also to the American tradition of combining European antiques and elements of old rooms in new, creative, and dramatic configurations. A series of tall windows on either side of the room, embellished with inventive hand-embroidered curtains by Lesage, resemble the long galleries of French and English houses. Centering the space is a neo-Palladian English mantel, so perennially popular in America, with an Italian Baroque mirror above. A seventeenth-century German chandelier hangs above the table over which a Turkish carpet drapes, evoking the period up until the mid-eighteenth century when Oriental rugs were first introduced in Europe and considered too valuable for the floors. The lofty proportions and all of the fantastic objects—the giltwood console and a portrait of Sir Richard Bourke by Gilbert Jackson—contribute to the power of the decor. Like Henry du Pont at Winterthur, Couturier alters his decoration with the changing seasons, using a set of 1710 Queen Anne chairs in the fall and winter and a lighter set of eighteenth-century Danish chairs in the spring and summer.

Both stylish and traditional, Couturier's design relies on formal symmetry and attenuated proportions to convey a sense of grandeur. The curtains, embroidered with large-scale abstracted flowers, bring the room into the twenty-first century.

197

LIVING ROOM, TRIBECA LOFT

NEW YORK CITY

Good modern rooms can certainly be created with ready-made designs, but it is difficult to make a truly memorable interior without at least some custom elements. With great aplomb, David Kleinberg works with the finest bespoke parts. He is famous for his modern and inventive eye and exacting attention to detail, which allow him to create truly innovative rooms.

Lofts are difficult to decorate because the space usually has little or no architectural personality. The formula, perfected by art galleries, of using pure white walls to display contemporary art, is very often translated into loft interiors. However, the owners of this loft asked Kleinberg to forego this model and create a more classical home-like setting. Kleinberg focused the room on an over-scaled backlit mantel of polished and chiseled limestone inlaid with bronze inspired by the work of Paul Dupré-Lafon, the French interior architect and Hermès product designer from the 1940s. A sculptural stair, composed of cantilevered blocks, with a cast-bronze balustrade of twining branches, pinecones, and seed pods was designed in collaboration with artist Bill Sullivan. Combined with Kleinberg's neutral palette and Wenge paneling, these bespoke aspects indeed make a memorable room.

The spare Art Deco quality of the balustrade harmonizes with the rectilinear wall paneling and the crisp geometry of the room.

The nineteenth-century-style Chesterfield sofas, renowned for their comfort, are an unusual choice for a modern room.

201

SITTING ROOM, ALBERT HADLEY APARTMENT

NEW YORK CITY

Albert Hadley was reticent for his New York apartment to be represented here because he felt it was not grand enough. But, while it is not a large space, Hadley's sitting room encapsulates the notion that refinement is not about size. In fact, the success of Hadley's room is created by its intimacy as well as by the play of patterns and voids that come together in a complete and artistic picture. On one wall there is an alcove with a day bed under a mirror. Opposite, a framed panel of turquoise serves as a centering device. All of the walls are covered in one of Hadley's signature patterns and the shiny brown lacquered ceiling highlights the regular geometry, uniting all the parts of the room and injecting a sense of expansiveness into the small space. The white-painted chairs and lacquered work table are light and effortless to rearrange, making it easier to move about the room and to use the space for different occasions. Hadley has also set the visual center relatively low, making the room welcoming and commodious. His works of art, many of them associated with some of the most important figures of twentieth-century American decoration, including Elsie de Wolfe, Van Day Truex, and Eleanor Brown, represent the continuum of great decorators among which Hadley can easily be counted. What makes this or any room fine? It is the sum of parts, whether elaborate or simple, novel or well-known, that in the end, as Hadley so remarkably demonstrates, is the tangible genius of its maker.

The gilt wood frame
of the turquoise
wall panel echoes
the gold surface of
the lamp and adds
subtle enrichment. A
drawing by Van Day
Truex, Hadley's great
friend, perfectly suits
the scale and personal
nature of the room.
In the corner of the
alcove, a simply framed
mirror reflects the
lacquered ceiling and
opposite wall.

PLACES TO VISIT

BASSETT HALL
Colonial Williamsburg
Williamsburg, Virginia

BEAUPORT
Historic New England
75 Eastern Point Boulevard
Gloucester, Massachusetts

THE ELMS
The Preservation Society of Newport County
367 Bellevue Avenue
Newport, Rhode Island

HAMILTON HOUSE
Historic New England
40 Vaughans Lane
South Berwick, Maine

HOLLYHOCK HOUSE
4800 Hollywood Boulevard
Los Angeles, California

ISABELLA STEWART GARDNER
MUSEUM
280 The Fenway
Boston, Massachusetts

KINGSCOTE
The Preservation Society of Newport County
253 Bellevue Avenue
Newport, Rhode Island

MAGNOLIA MOUND PLANTATION
2161 Nicholson Drive
Baton Rouge, Louisiana

MARK TWAIN HOUSE & MUSEUM
351 Farmington Avenue
Hartford, Connecticut

MONTICELLO
Thomas Jefferson Foundation
931 Thomas Jefferson Highway
Charlottesville, Virginia

MOUNT VERNON ESTATE
& GARDENS
3200 Mount Vernon Memorial Highway
Mount Vernon, Virginia

SAARINEN HOUSE & GARDEN
Cranbrook Art Museum
39221 Woodward Avenue
Bloomfield Hills, Michigan

VICTORIA MANSION
109 Danforth Street
Portland, Maine

VIZCAYA MUSEUM & GARDENS
3251 South Miami Avenue
Miami, Florida

WINTERTHUR MUSEUM &
COUNTRY ESTATE
5105 Kennett Pike
Winterthur, Delaware

ACKNOWLEDGMENTS

Clearly, a project of this breadth relies on the wisdom and generosity of many people, all of whom I cannot practically thank. However, I am most grateful for the participation of the owners of rooms, architects, decorators, other designers, and photographers represented here, and the many people who offered their insights and suggestions. That old phrase rings true: "words cannot begin to express" my thanks to so many for so much.

It is most important that I attempt to express my gratitude to my partner, Rick Ellis. This is our twenty-fifth year together, and it is an understatement to say that his encouragement and keen opinions over the past quarter century were essential to the writing of this book.

Within the design community, I would like to acknowledge the special help of the editors and authors who freely shared their opinions about quality and interior decoration: Cindy Allen, Sian Ballen, Louis Bofferding, Pamela Fiori, Howard Christian, Cynthia Conigliaro, Elaine Greenstein, Albert Hadley, William Irvine, Eric Kahn, Jim Larkin, Jane Daniels Lear, Todd Longstaff-Gowan, Sarah Medford, Mitchell Owens, Julia Reed, Deb Shriver, Jeanne Sloane, Pilar Viladas, and Bunny Williams.

I also have an important debt to museum presidents, directors, and curators, who aided this study. I offer my thanks especially to Leslie Greene Bowman, Julia Burke, Stephen Calloway, Morrison Heckscher, Tim Knox, Maggie Lidz, Amelia Peck, Thomas Michie, David Revere McFadden, Margaret Pritchard, J. Thomas Savage Jr., Richard Nylander, Robert Leath, Paul Miller, Steven Miller, Cynthia O'Malley, and Susan Owens.

I offer profound thanks to Nancy Romeu of our interior design practice and all of our colleagues and patrons at the Jayne Design Studio. Their constant interest and good humored support helped bring this book to fruition.

Stephen Gerth, rector of Saint Mary the Virgin Church in New York City, offered moral and intellectual support.

It is a great pleasure to acknowledge the creative team that has given The Finest Rooms its form. Anne Walker researched and helped to write the text, creating an important foundation for the book. Elizabeth White at The Monacelli Press encouraged the notion of this volume, and her skill as an editor is manifested in its pages. I am particularly grateful to photographers Kerri McCaffety and Jeffrey Hirsch. This most handsome presentation is the work of designer Susan Evans of Design per se.

Library of Congress Control Number 2010931299

ISBN 978-158093-242-4

Designed by Susan Evans, Design per se, Inc.

Printed in China

www.monacellipress.com

10 9 8 7 6 5 4 3 2 1

Photography Credits:

Peter Aaron: 13

© William Abranowicz / Art + Commerce: 78, 79

Michel Arnaud: 126, 127, 128, 129

Alexandre Bailhache: 154–155, 156, 157

John Blais: 94, 97 top

David Bohl, courtesy of The Preservation Society of Newport County: 36, 40

Antoine Bootz: 152

Steven Brooke: 50

© Langdon Clay/Esto: 2, 16 bottom

The Colonial Williamsburg Foundation. Photo by Craig MacDougal: 66, 68, 69

© Cranbrook Art Museum/ Balthazar Korab: 58, 60, 61

Grey Crawford: 176, 177, 178, 179

Kurt A. Dolnier: 41

© 2010 Eames Office, LLC (eamesoffice.com), photographer Michael Freeman: 80

© 2010 Eames Office, LLC (eamesoffice.com), photographer Timothy Street-Porter: 82, 83

Pieter Estersohn: 7 bottom right, 198, 199, 200, 201

Scott Frances: 132, 133, 134–135, 148, 150–151, 172, 174–175, 180, 181, 182–183

Oberto Gili: 8, 84, 85

Francois Halard / Trish South Management/ trunkarchive.com: 144, 145, 146, 147

John M. Hall: 90, 92, 93

Reto Halme: 12 right

Lizzie Himmel: 7 left, 104, 105, 106, 107

Jeffrey Hirsch/NEW YORK SOCIALDIARY.COM: 98, 99, 108, 109, 110, 111, 112, 113, 114–115, 116, 117, 118–119

Courtesy of Historic New England: 4 center, 46, 47, 48–49

Paula Illingworth: 140, 141

Isabella Stewart Gardner Museum, Boston: 42

Isabella Stewart Gardner Museum, Boston. Photo by Clements / Howcroft Photography, 2008: 43

Isabella Stewart Gardner Museum, Boston. Photo by Thomas Lingner, 2008: 44–45

Nathan Kirkman: 196–197

Erik Kvalsvik: 4 top, 18, 20, 21

Fred Lyon: 70, 71, 72–73

The Mark Twain House & Museum, Hartford, CT: 32, 34–35

Kerri McCaffety: Cover and back cover, 11, 26, 27, 28, 29, 86, 88, 89, 100, 101, 102, 103, 120, 122–123, 124, 125, 143, 158, 160, 161, 162, 163, 165, 166–167, 184, 185, 186, 187, 202, 203, 204, 205

Menil Archives, The Menil Collection, Houston 05.3363: Menil home, interior view of the living room, 1982. Photo by Hickey-Robertson: 76–77

07.3363: Menil home, interior view of the living room, 1964. Photo by Balthazar Korab: 74

Monticello/photograph by Roger Straus III: 17

Monticello/photograph by Robert Lautman: 16

Courtesy of the Mount Vernon Ladies' Association: 25

Courtesy of the Mount Vernon Ladies' Association. Photograph by Gavin Ashworth: 23

Courtesy of the Mount Vernon Ladies' Association. Photograph by Hal Conroy: 24

Peter Murdock: 188, 189, 190, 191

Dan Piassick: 136, 137, 138–139

Paul Rocheleau: 14

© Roberto Schezen/Esto: 51

Tim Street-Porter: 7 top right, 130, 131, 194

© Tim Street-Porter/Esto: 52

Larry Underhill: 54–55

Simon Upton / The Interior Archive: 96, 97 bottom, 142, 192, 193

Brian Vanden Brink: 31, 56, 57

Victoria Mansion (The Morse-Libby House), Portland, Maine. Photo by J. David Bohl: 30

Fritz von der Schulenberg: 168, 170, 171

Jonathan Wallen: 12 left, 37, 38, 39

Courtesy, Winterthur: 62, 64, 65